On Talking Terms With Dogs: Calming Signals

by Turid Rugaas

Introduction by Terry Ryan

Copyright April 1997 by Turid Rugaas and Terry Ryan

Author:
Turid Rugaas
Boks 109
N-3360 Geithus, Norway

Publisher:
Legacy By Mail, Inc.
PO Box 697
Carlsborg, WA 98324
USA

Phone: 360-683-9646
Fax: 360-683-5755
Toll-free Phone: 888-876-9364
Toll-free Fax: 800-509-9814
E-mail: info@legacybymail.com
Web Page: www.legacybymail.com

To order this book and other publications, or to request
a catalog, contact Legacy by Mail at the above address.

My everlasting gratitude and love to VESLA,
who started it all, just by being herself.

Contents

Vesla's Story

The big Briard attacked violently and with a roar. At full speed he went for the little Elkhound, who stopped moving, stood quite still, and turned her head to one side. Just a few feet away from the Elkhound, the Briard stopped and looked bewildered, as if he didn't know what to do. Then he started to look around for some replacement activity, sniffed a little at the ground, and turned back to base.

The place was my training field. The client was a Briard with dog-to-dog problems. The little Elkhound was my own Vesla, thirteen years of age.

Vesla always knows what to do and she always manages to calm down other dogs, whether they are aggressive, afraid, stressed or just harassing. For eleven years no dog has been able to throw her off her mental balance. She is the picture of a survivor, a conflict-solving dog with all the communication skills needed to survive.

Vesla wasn't always like that. She came to me as a stray dog, and we meant to re-home her, as she upset my own dogs with her aggressive and violent behaviour. She fought, she quarreled, she was stressed, she was impossible, and I didn't feel for starting to work with her. But nobody wanted her, so with a sigh we kept her, and started to try to incorporate her into the family of people and dogs.

It was a time of trials. I am sure she was the worst dog I have ever had in the house. But gradually things got better. She stopped climbing the curtains. She could go for walks without trying to bite the others all the time. She could relax now and then.

And then one day I saw to my astonishment that she actually started to communicate with the other dogs. Their work had started to get through to her! When I discovered that she actually was getting back her dog language, I tried my usual method for training. I praised every step in the right direction, every time she had a glimpse of a calming signal, I praised her. She got better and better. I realized to my surprise that it was possible to reinforce her own language by praising, and then things happened very fast. She was now helped by both my dogs and me. In a very short time she was a miracle of dog language. One year after I got her, she had stopped all her aggressive behaviour, and from then until today, twelve years later, she has not once been in trouble with any dog. They just cannot make her loose control.

The story of Vesla made me realize that it is possible to teach back lost language to dogs. Since then I have made this teaching a life-style and my main job. And it has enriched my life, as I now understand better, see better, what dogs feel. I truly feel that I am on talking terms with the dogs. And that gives me a good feeling, just like the childhood dream about talking to animals.

Thank you Vesla, for all you taught me. It changed my life.

Introduction by Terry Ryan

The occasion was "Animals and Us," the Sixth International Conference on Human-Animal Interactions in Montreal. A quiet, polite seminar attendee, Turid Rugaas, sat a couple of rows ahead of me during the canine behavior sessions. Turid should never play poker. I couldn't help but notice her shoulders tensing up or relaxing depending on the speaker. The funny thing was, her body language was directly reflecting my own opinion of the various speakers' presentations.

Networking! That's what symposiums are all about! I wanted to meet this stranger from overseas whose response to behavior issues seemed to so closely mirror my own. Realizing that English was not her native tongue, and wondering if she would understand, it took me until the end of the day to gather the nerve to approach her. Since that meeting back in 1992, I have spent a lot of time with Turid. I've invited her to present at my behavior and training camps and seminars both in the United States and overseas. She has captivated her audiences where ever she goes. She was a big hit in Japan with her blue eyes and flaxen braids!

Turid's farm, Hagan Hundeskole, is located on a heavily forested mountain top overlooking scenic fjords of Norway. People from all over the country bring their dogs for her instruction in basic manners and rehabilitation of problem behaviors. I have been there to observe during her work with dogs and she has amazed me. The stories she tells in this book are true. I have come to realize that she is on the cutting edge of understanding canine behavior. The following quote gives the essence of Turid Rugaas's theory on calming signals.

Dogs, being flock animals, have a language for communication with each other. Canine language in general consists of a large variety of signals using body, face, ears, tail, sounds, movement, and expression. The dog's innate ability to signal is easily lost or reinforced through life's experience. If we study the signals dogs use with each other and use them ourselves, we increase our ability to communicate with our dogs. Most noteworthy of all canine signals are the calming signals, which are used to maintain a healthy social hierarchy and resolution of conflict within the flock. These are skills which, when carried over to our own interactions with dogs, can be highly beneficial to our relationship. Dogs have the ability to calm themselves in the face of a shock (fearful or stressful situation) and to calm each other as well. As an example let's consider the manner in which dogs meet each other. Dogs which are worried in a social situation can communicate concepts such as, 'I know you are the boss around here and I won't make trouble.' Furthermore, the boss dog is very apt to want the worried dog to realize that no trouble is intended. 'Don't worry, I'm in charge around here and I mean you no harm.' Dogs that do not signal properly can be the cause of problems.

I've asked Turid to write it down. Like many dedicated dog enthusiasts, she's been too busy **doing it** to **write about it**. The brief chapters that follow are a direct translation from Turid's Norwegian concepts. The terms and mannerisms have been kept the same, with no attempt to change syntax to fit within English norms. This is a conscience decision on my part, with Turid's permission. When trying to communicate in a different language, one finds that often there's just not a comparable word or meaning for the thought. Let's take ourselves away from established language and the barriers a language imposes. Subordinance displays, displacement activities, rituals, drives–let's set aside our own labels and opinions and just talk about what we see–and for a few moments think about canine body language as Turid Rugaas does.

Terry Ryan: On trips to Europe I make it a point to visit Turid's farm, Hagan Hundeskole, to observe her work. I have been on seminar tours with her in Europe, USA and Japan. Whether a training camp north of the arctic circle or a national symposium in Geneva, each time she has left me favorably impressed with her ability to explain to her audience what is going on with a dog at any given time. She is among the first in her country to take a special interest in "street mixes"–the common Norwegian term for random bred dogs. In Scandinavia she is championing the move away from, to again use Norwegian terms, the "frying pan" method of dog training and advocating "contact training."

Chapter I

Calming Signals—The Life Insurance Policy

In books about wolves you will find the body language of wolves described as "cutoff" signals, as the observers of them saw how they were cutting off aggression in other wolves. These signals have been described for years and are well known. The same people describing these signals seem to think that dogs do not have the same ability to cutoff aggressions in each other (Michael Fox: *Behavior of Wolves, Dogs and Related Canids*)–and how wrong they were! Dogs have the same ability and the same social skills to avoid conflicts as the wolves have. Maybe the people did not see it because the wolves are much more intense in their behavior, due to their life situation. Dogs, that is domesticated dogs, are much more subtle in their skills and use much smaller letters, so to say. They are usually not in the same position of danger as wolves, and they need not be so much speaking in big letters to each other.

Prevention

When I started to observe and use these signals, I called them calming signals. Cutoff is not the appropriate word, as they are used much more as prevention than really cutting off something. The signals are used at an early state to prevent things from happening, avoiding threats from people and dogs, calming down nervousness, fear, noise, and unpleasant things. The signals are used for calming themselves when they feel stressed or uneasy. The signals are used to make the others involved feel safer and understand the goodwill the signals tell about. They are used to make friends with other dogs and people.

1

Conflict solving

Dogs who had the possibility of developing communication skills with other dogs, and were not losing the signals because of us, would understand each other and actually never be in conflict with others. Wolves and dogs try to avoid conflicts. They are conflict-solving animals. It is usually us, the human species, who make conflicts between us and our dogs.

We shall look upon the signals–what they are, how they are used–and how you can learn to understand your dog better and be a better leader for your dog. It will help you in training and handling, and I trust that these new skills will enrich your life as they have mine.

How did it start?

I knew about the cutoff signals and had also observed that dogs calmed each other. I did not know that it was possible to make dogs learn again language lost, or that it was possible to use the same language as dogs, to make them understand me better.

When Vesla, the stray dog (her name means "Little One" by the way), showed me that it was possible to learn the language, I wanted to know if people could help dogs to a better language and how it worked.

Together with a colleague, Ståle Ødegaard, I started a project that took us one year and a half to complete. During that time we trained dogs, observed dogs, took pictures, slides, videos and gathered much information and knowledge. At the end of that period I felt pretty sure I understood how it was working, and I had already used it in training my dogs and had seen that it worked. This documentation gave me the strength to act on my convictions, and I then started work with the rehabilitation of dogs.

Today I spend much time teaching others to see, understand and use the calming signals of dogs. How does it work? Think about an average day with your dog. You get up in the morning, with a little tiny bit of morning sour, and tell the dog off with a little annoyance in your voice. He turns his face sidewise to you, and licks his nose in one quick movement. You finish morning toilet and dressing, and you go to the door. The dog is happy to come out and fusses around you. You command him SIT. The commanding tone makes your dog yawn before he sits down. You go out the door, he pulls a little and you jerk him back, he then turns his back on you and puts his nose to the ground. At the park you let him loose for a few minutes, and then your wrist watch tells you to go back. You call for your dog. Was your voice a little stressed? Your dog starts moving towards you slowly and in a curve. You think he does it to annoy you, and you yell at him. He sniffs the ground, curves even more, and looks away from you. He finally comes and you scold him or, even worse, you shake him up. He turns his face from you, licking his nose or yawning.

This was only the morning procedures. We could have gone through the whole day like this and told you step by step every time your dog tries to calm you down with his signals. The signals are there as soon as things happen.

Dogs use the signals as soon as there is anything to calm down. If they awake, they "talk." Just like you and me.

Often the signals come in quick movements, so quick that we need to really look to see them. By experience you learn to see these small flashes. Other dogs see them, even other animals, like cats. All it takes is a little practice and knowing what to look for.

Which dogs have these signals?

The wolves have them. The dogs inherited them. All the different breeds all over the world, no matter which size, color, or shape they took. They all have them. It is a truly universal language and a wonderful one because it means we can communicate with dogs wherever we meet them.

Just imagine being able to travel the world, and everywhere you go you can speak your native tongue, and everybody else speaks the same language. How marvelous that would be. I have been to USA, Japan, England, and other countries, and I have seen it by my own eyes. The dogs speak the same language all over the world.

Some breeds have more of some signals than of others, due to a different outlook. Black dogs for instance have a tendency to use licking more than other facial expression, though they will understand other breeds using other signals and they will understand you using them.

Dogs and wolves have strong instincts for conflict solving, communication and cooperation.

Their repertoire also includes threatening signals, and when we are dealing with dogs we have a choice of how to behave: we can be calming, friendly, reassuring, or we can be threatening. Whatever we choose will have consequences for our relationship to the dog. When you are using threats to your dog, intentionally or unintentionally, the dog will try to calm you back. For the conflict solving dog, threats must be calmed down. I prefer to put it this way: Why on earth should we ever use threatening signals to dogs?

What signals we are talking about? We know about 28 or 29 signals. Some signals are used for other things as well, in other situations. Some are so swift that we can hardly see them. It takes experience to see it all in every situation. But by experience and lots of observations you will be able to catch the glimpse of them all, and you will at all times be able to tell how your dog is feeling. You will understand your dog much better. And isn't that what we all want? To really know how they feel?

"The social dynamics of a wolf pack is often used as a model for dog-dog and dog-human interactions. I have seen dog people (and some wolf people as well) caught up in the idea of always maintaining high rank by aggressive means, believing their only choices are between forcibly dominating the animal or submitting to it. The problem with this approach is two-fold. First, aggression may well escalate, and second, an either-or choice between forcible dominance or submission is not the only choice available to wolves, to dogs or to humans.

With what she calls "calming signals," based on canine expressive behavior, Turid Rugaas introduces dog trainers and owners to another option to try to improve relationships between humans and their dogs and between dogs and other dogs."

Pat Goodmann, Wolf Park

Chapter II

Calming Signals: How to Identify and Use Them.

Turning of the head

A signal can be a swift movement, turning his head to the side and back, or the head can be held to the side for some time. It can be just a tiny movement, or the whole head clearly to the side.

Your dog may use head turning when another dog is approaching him to tell the other dog to calm down. Maybe your dog was approached too fast, or directly head on instead of in a curve. His head may turn if you stoop over him. Maybe he stands still, but turns his head, which tells you about his discomfort in the situation.

You can use head turning yourself when a dog starts to get worried or frightened when you approach him. When a scared dog starts to bark or growl at you, turn your head.

For example: When two dogs meet, they both look away for a second, and then they greet each other happily. Or when I go up to my dog Saga to take her picture, she finds the camera a bit scary. She looks away when I take the picture, but looks at me again when I remove the camera from my face.

Not turning the head, but allowing the eyes only to slide to the side and look away to avert the direct stare is a signal similar to head turning. Your dog may use it when another is approaching him or when you stare at your dog or approach him front to front.

You can use it when a dog approaches you and you have difficulties in turning your head for some reason.

For example: Ulla is in her yard with me, and a male dog comes visiting. He is a very self assured dog, and friendly, so he goes straight towards her without turning his head, curving or anything. Ulla still stands there wagging her tail, because his eyes are flicking from side to side as he approaches her. She understands the message, he is a friendly guy.

Shortening the eye by making the eyes look at another individual in a softer way, lowering lids, and not staring in a threatening way are signals. Your dog may use them when he looks at someone straight on, and still does not want to threaten. You can use them when you are training the exercise "eye contact," making the contact softer and more friendly.

For example: Sitting down with your eyes at the same level as the dog might be threatening for some dogs. When you feel that he actually feels threatened by it, you can stand up and look at him from above, that way your eyes are "shortened" and less staring. Many dogs find it difficult to get someone's face straight on to their own.

Turning away

Turning the side or back to someone is very calming. When dogs play wildly, some of them will start turning their side or back in between playing, to make things calm down a little.

Your dog may use it when another dog growls at him or behaves threatening in some way, like running up too fast, or when you use a very cross voice or go up to him when he feels that you are angry. When young dogs pester older ones, the older often turns back to make them calm down. When you jerk at the leash your dog may turn away from you, maybe pulling even more.

You can use it when a dog shows signs of nervousness or aggressiveness to you. If he jumps at you, turn away, and he will most times stop.

For example: Julias, a Tibetan Mastiff, turned first his head, then side, and finally his back to a very angry German Shepherd. When he had his back to her, she actually became calmer.

If your dog is overwhelmingly jumping and nagging you, turn your back on the dog. If you are approaching a strange dog, and suddenly you see that the dog is getting nervous, turn your back to him. In a few seconds the dog will come to you.

For example: Gino, a Doberman Pinscher, was not happy with young boys, they had been pestering him a good deal. The owner taught the boys to turn their backs to Gino, and then Gino came up to them and made friends.

Licking nose

A very quick movement of the tongue, so quick that sometimes it is hard to see is a calming signal.

Your dog may use it when approaching another dog. When you bend over your dog or hold him tight, and when you bend down to grab him or talk to him in an angry voice, he may use this signal.

You cannot really use it. It is one of the signals I find awkward for people to use.

For example: I bend over Vesla to clean her ears. She looks away and licks. The veterinarian bends down to lift Ulla up on the table. She licks.

Rocky sees another dog in the distance coming his way. He stops, turns his head and licks several times.

Freezing

Your dog will freeze, stop, stand, sit or lie still, without moving a muscle when a much bigger dog comes up too close and starts sniffing him all over.

For example: Lorry, a little Whippet, was greeted by a very big German Shepherd male, who sniffed him all over. He stood as still as he could, freezing completely, until the dog started for other "prey." Then he could move again.

A man training his dog for obedience got angry when his very young dog ran out of a long down to see some other dogs approaching in the distance. The man got very angry and started to yell with real aggression in his voice. The dog stopped and stood quite still. He didn't dare to move. The man ran up to him and really gave him the treatment for being so "stubborn."

A competitor got a new dog for competition work, and being very ambitious of having a champion at an early age, he started training and correcting the puppy. Then one day when he called the dog, the dog stopped, sat down and didn't move.

Walking slowly, using slow movements

Movements that get slower, sometimes so slow that there is hardly any movement at all have a very calming effect.

Your dog may use it when another dog is seen. The slow movements start at the sight of the other dog. They start when you call for your dog, and you are a bit irritable or commanding in your voice. They start when there are a lot of things happening around the dog, and he tries to calm things down. When you jump and wave and scream a lot to make the dog run faster, you will often get the opposite. The dog gets slower to calm you down.

You can use it when a dog seems frightened of you, or when you do not want to scare a dog. When you go up to a dog that you want to put a leash on. The slower you move, the better chance of making him stand still.

For example: Shiba, a Border Collie agility dog, got slower and slower on the agility course. The owner ran around, jumped up and down, waved her arms and yelled a lot to encourage the dog. In the end, Shiba hardly moved around the agility field because she was trying to calm her owner.

The owner is calling Candy to go home from the park. Some people and dogs stand between her and her owner, so Candy walks slowly past them before she continues to her owner.

You say "down" in a harsh way. Your dog gets down, but very slowly, because he has to calm the anger in your voice.

Play position

Going down with front legs in a bowing position can be an invitation to play, if the dog is moving legs from side to side in a playful manner. If he stands still, in a bow, the possibility for it being a calming signal is high.

Your dog may use this when he wants to become friends with another dog who is a little skeptical or nervous. He may use the bow when he meets another animal (horse or cow) he does not feel too sure about.

You can use it by stretching your arms, like when you yawn, but stretch down.

For example: Vesla wanted a St. Bernard dog to feel safe with her, so after having walked slowly towards him, turning her head from side to side, she stopped at some distance and went down in play position. She stood there for some seconds, until Buster felt safe with her, and did the same to answer her signal.

Little Pip the Chihuahua was scared of bigger dogs. When Saga came along, Pip went down in play position to make sure that Saga would be polite and nice to her. Saga answered her signal by moving slower, in a curve, and looking away.

Prince, a Rottweiler, went down in play position when he met a little bit frightened Golden Retriever girl. He stood there for many minutes, quite still, to make her feel better about him being there.

Sitting down

Either turning back to you while sitting down, or just sitting down when a dog is approaching is a signal.

Your dog may use it when another dog is making him feel uncertain or when you yell to make him come.

You can use it. Sit when your dog is stressed and cannot relax. Make your guests sit down if you have a dog who is not quite sure about strangers.

For example: Roscoe, a German Shepherd, turned his back to his owner and sat down when the command came. It was said in a very strong voice, and it evidently made the dog feel uncomfortable. I made the owner talk to his dog in a normal, everyday voice, and the dog came to him.

Saga was out with me the other day, when suddenly two fiercely barking strange dogs came running towards her. She is best at facial expressions, but it was getting dark so she had to be more clear about it. She sat down as they came rushing. They immediately slowed down, stopped barking, and came up to her, sniffing the ground. Saga is never in trouble with other dogs. She is very sure about how to handle any situation.

Down

Lying down on his back, belly up, is submission. Lying down with belly to the ground is a calming act. It is a very strong one too, often used by high ranking dogs like my Ulla, who is leader of the pack.

Your dog may use it as a puppy when playing gets too rough or as an adult when young ones seem to be scared of him. When they get tired during play and want the others to calm down they may use it.

You can use it when your dog is stressed and nagging you. Lie down on the sofa. When a dog is feeling scared of you and not daring to come closer, lie down. In many cases he'll be right there.

For example: A bunch of dogs were playing in my training field and some of them were getting a bit overwhelming. Ulla went to the middle of the field, went down, and looked sphinx-like to the others. In a matter of minutes, they calmed down and also lay down around her.

A little scared dog didn't dare to approach Saga, who went into a down when she saw the fear. In a little while the other dared to make contact. An adult dog was together with five puppies, and they harassed him, obviously thinking he was a recirculated toy. He was patient with them. But when they started to get real mean, he got down, and they actually let him be and ran for each other instead. When he got up, they were at him once again.

Yawning

Yawning is probably the most intriguing of the signals, at least people seem to enjoy using it.

Your dog may yawn when you go into the veterinarian's office, when you fight or quarrel in the family, when you hold your dog too tight when a child comes up to hug him, and a million other situations.

You can use it when your dog feels uncertain, a little bit scared, stressed, worried, or when you want him to calm down a bit.

For example: Ulla is easily heated up when someone is running or playing. Playing with her might end with her biting at my trouser legs. When she starts to get excited, I stand still and yawn a little, and she relaxes.

My colleague Ståle came to my house when I was having a client with a fearful dog. Ståle came in the door, saw immediately the dog's fear, stopped and yawned several times. The dog looked interested at him, then turned to me, and I yawned too. In a matter of minutes the dog was quite comfortable with us and took contact.

Candy was restless and stressed one evening, and the owner sat down, yawning. Candy eventually stopped her restless wandering, laid down by the owner's feet, and relaxed.

Little Sheila was loved very much by her owner. Once when I was there the owner took Sheila on her lap and hugged her. Dogs feel uncomfortable in such a tight situation, so Sheila yawned and yawned.

Sniffing

Sniffing can be a swift movement down to the ground or the floor, and up again, or it can be persistently standing there for some time until the problem situation is over. As dogs also sniff to actually sniff smells, one has to see the whole situation to be sure what it is.

Your dog may use it when another dog is approaching him, when someone is walking straight at him, or when a sudden situation occurs–for instance two dogs very suddenly being too close. When you walk along the road and someone is walking directly at you, maybe carrying a big hat or something, your dog may sniff. When you call your dog and you are a bit annoyed or commanding in your voice, or maybe standing with full front to the dog, your dog will sniff several times while coming.

You cannot really use it. I find it hard to practice sniffing. But something like it can be used; you sitting down, scratching the grass or something.

I have a lot of wonderful sniffing examples–dogs seem to use it a lot when they communicate.

A client with a very aggressive dog came to me. She didn't dare to have him out of the car, as she was afraid he would kill any dog outside. I took Vesla with me, and let her go by her own outside the car. I told the owner to hold the leash and open the door of the car, letting the "aggressive" dog out. And out he came–a monster of little golden mix breed, all teeth, and foaming and barking his head off. He really looked fierceful. Vesla was only yards away, and when King came out of the car door like a rocket, she just put her nose to the ground and kept it there. King was snarling and acting wildly. Vesla was sniffing, but suddenly she made up her mind, went straight up to him, nose to nose, and King fell like a punctured balloon. Ten minutes later he ran happily with seven other dogs in the training field.

When I walked with Ulla down in the village the other day, a man came towards us with a barking little dog on a leash. Ulla went to the side of the road, put her nose to the ground, and stood there as they approached and passed.

Candy was called by her owner in the park, and she ran happily after him. Suddenly another dog came up to her. Candy slowed down, sniffed the ground, the other dog went on his way, and she continued her happy running to her master.

Sara, a Doberman Pinscher, was tied to a tree while her owner did something else. A man came towards her, and she immediately turned side to him started to sniff the ground. She felt uncomfortable by a stranger coming up to her while she was tied up, and tried to make him understand that. He did not, but I managed to stop him for her.

Curving or walking in a curve or a little away from another dog or a person is a signal. Dogs do not usually go straight toward each other. They might, if they use other clear signals, but it is impolite to do so and most of them try to avoid it.

Your dog may do it when you meet someone coming towards you on the path. When something is in the dog's way, and he needs to go that way. When you walk with your dog in heel position and something comes against him on that side, he might try to walk on the other side of you. When a dog looks fearful or angry, your dog will use a wide curve around him to calm him down.

You can use it when approaching a fearful or aggressive dog. When you meet a dog who gives you a calming signal like sniffing, licking, head turning, or something else. Sometimes you need to use a wide curve, sometimes it is enough to change direction a tiny bit, just walking slightly to the side of the dog. Watch the dog you are meeting, and curve as much as necessary to make the dog feel comfortable.

For example: Candy met a Newfoundland puppy who was not very acquainted with other dogs and felt scared of her. Candy immediately walked around him in a wide curve, her nose to the ground. Max met another male out walking and went in a curve past him.

A German Wirehair Pointer named Connie was with her owners at my place, and because they said she was scared of people, I came walking across the room towards her. When she licked and looked away, I changed direction, and looked away from her, and passed her only feet away, but curving. She came up to me right away and took contact.

Splitting up

Going physically between dogs or people is a signal. When dogs or humans or a dog and a human get too tight, and the situation might be tense, many dogs go between to split up and to avoid any conflict.

Your dog may do it when you take a child on your lap and do a lot of fussing with it, when you waltz around with someone, or when you sit

13

tight together with your friend on the sofa. When two dogs start to be a little tense and being too tight, they may use this signal.

You can do it when dogs get tense, when your dog gets uneasy or frightened in a situation, and when children do things to dogs that make them feel uneasy.

For example: In a puppy class some of the bigger puppies started to be a little bit too tough with one of the smaller ones. Before I had the chance of doing anything about it, Saga went between them and took care of the small puppy. The others were not allowed close to it.

Two adult dogs were playing rather wildly, and a puppy in the same room felt uneasy about it and hid under the owner's chair. Every time they came toward the puppy, he whined. Another adult dog, a Springer Spaniel named Dennis, came in the door and went right over to split them up and protect the little one. He stood beside the puppy, his side to the others, not allowing them close.

I was out walking Saga when we met a little Poodle. Suddenly a Samoyed came roaring, attacking the Poodle. Saga went right in between them and stopped the attack.

Wagging tail

A wagging tail is not always a sign of happiness. You must look at the whole dog. If the dog is crawling towards you, whining and peeing, the wagging tail is a "white flag," trying to make you calm down.

Your dog will use it when you have lost your temper. The dog tries to make you calm down and be nice again.

You might not be able to use it. I have never been able to do so very effectively.

For example: Lobo's owner came home and had a worried look in his face, as Lobo had chewed up something the previous day, and he was worried it had happened again. The worried brow made Lobo crawl and wag his tail wildly, in the hope that his owner might look less angry.

My daughter had yelled at her twin daughters. When she came into the yard where Saga was, Saga came up to her with a wildly wagging tail and smiling all she could to make her calm down.

14

Cora, a German Shepherd, always greeted her owner by crawling, peeing and wagging tail. The owner had used a lot of scruff shaking, yelling and pinching ears. Cora was afraid of him every time she saw him, and her way of greeting him showed fear and also that she desperately tried to calm him.

There's more

The signals listed above are the most commonly used signals in dogs. But dogs also calm others by playing puppy by making themselves small, trying to lick faces, they can blink their eyes, smack their lips, and lift their paws.

For example: I had right in front of me a very aggressive Rottweiler who, by the sound of the deep growling, meant business and least no interference in his privacy. The growling became deeper if I tried to move my head or something, so I had to stand still. I was certainly not going to back up, so all I could think of doing was blinking my eyes. After a while the growling ceased, and suddenly his tail started to wag a little. It took me very shortly to become his friend.

A little scared Basenji growled at a German Shepherd, who stood still lifting his paw up and down, licking his nose and blinking his eyes. And he succeeded in making the Basenji calm down.

These are all calming signals. Dogs also have other signals; some are threatening, like staring, walking straight on to someone, stooping over, growling, barking, attacking and showing teeth. Some only tell us about excitement inside the dog; those are hackles and tails.

These signals are often misinterpreted, as they are easy to see and are what people look at. They tell us something about the dog's excitement in that situation, but don't be too occupied with them. Look for other signals– threatening or calming. They will tell you more.

Observation skills

It is important to be able to see these signals in your own and other dogs. It is important for you to be able to help your dog, using the signals yourself, know them well enough to identify them when they happen.

If you have not been very much aware of them before, you can teach yourself the skill of seeing them, by training yourself.

At home

Spend some time at home sitting and just observing your dog. In a quiet home atmosphere you will not get many signals, but do so anyway as a start. Someone moving, going around the house, guests coming–something will happen during that time, and then you can observe what your dog is doing.

With other dogs

Then make use of every situation where your dog is meeting other dogs. In the park maybe, or somewhere where they are off leash, then you can concentrate on what your dog is doing. Every time your dog meets another dog, look at him the second he sees the other dog at a distance, and notice which signals he is using.

One at a time

A third way of observing is to decide on one signal you want to be able to identify. Maybe you have already noticed some signals your dog is using. Maybe you recall that you have seen him licking now and then, or yawning. Then decide, for the next weeks I will try to see licking every time I see a dog. Just keep an eye on the dogs being there, to see if the licking occurs. It takes some concentration from your side in the beginning, but it becomes almost automatic.

When you feel sure that you see licking when it happens and can understand how the dog is using it, then start observing one or two signals more. Observe head turning, since that occurs very often, and maybe curving or sniffing.

In a rather short time you will find yourself reading all dogs you see. It becomes a kind of an interesting hobby you get more and more hooked on to the more you do it.

Welcome to the world of dog language!

Chapter III

Case Histories

Story One - Pippi

Pippi was a German Shorthaired Pointer, five years old, and her owner stopped down the road, not daring to come closer. She came to me with her dog, which she thought was dangerously aggressive to other dogs. Pippi looked calm and nice, greeted me nicely, and seemed to be a dog you can live with. Her owner looked pale and stressed, and said that she was scared about what we were going to do.

I told her shortly what I was about to do, and she turned even paler, looking like she was going to faint. I told her to stand still, not say anything, not do anything, and that she could give me the leash if she wanted to. No, she wanted to hold Pippi herself. And then I called for Vesla, who had been waiting around the corner of the house, and she came. The second Pippi saw her she was about to start attacking and barking. Vesla had in a glimpse taken the whole situation into consideration, stopped and stood still for a second with her nose to the ground. This made Pippi stand still instead of leaping. Then slowly she started to move in curves towards Pippi, nose to the ground, her side always to Pippi. Vesla's language was so clear that Pippi stood fascinated looking at her instead of doing any attacks. Getting closer, Vesla became even slower and the last yards took several minutes to cross. Pippi then put her nose to the ground too, and there they stood, sniffing the same spot, without looking at each other.

The owner came back several months later. She came in the middle of a lesson, so I had a bunch of puppies around. Pippi was let out of the car, went quietly over to one of the puppies and licked him. She had changed her attitude to other dogs completely.

This is a typical Vesla story. For twelve years she has changed the lives of dogs who no longer could communicate with others.

Buster, the big St. Bernard dog, was afraid of other dogs. Whenever he saw one, he hid behind his owner and had a real worried look in his face. Buster and his owner stood waiting for us on the path down to my farm when I let Vesla, my little Elkhound out. She spotted the other dog up the path and ran up to meet him, being fond of every other dog she met. But then she saw something in the other dog's face, eyes or attitude that made her change her happy tactic. She stopped running happily against him with a wagging tail. She started to move slowly, while her head turned slowly and very distinctly from side to side as she walked, using no direct eye contact, no speed. The big dog stood there, evidently getting the message she gave him, and some twenty feet away she stopped, went down stretching front legs in what we call playing position, only this time it was not to invite for playing. She just stood there until she saw something in his eyes that invited her to go even closer. He did not make any retreat, he just watched her. Then suddenly he too went down stretching front legs, and within seconds they had direct contact.

Vesla saw his worries, understood what to do, and did her job, making him feel less worried. They communicated, they understood each other, and therefore could solve the problem–being afraid.

Dogs are experts at this. Conflict solving is a part of their heritage from their ancestors the wolves, and they read each other like we read books. It is a part of their survival instincts and pack behavior. We will never be as good at it as the dogs are, but we can understand more about what they are telling us. We can observe, understand, and let the dog know we understand. We can give signals back to reassure them we understand. We can communicate better during training and daily life together with our dog.

We can learn their language in order to communicate better and do a better job with our dogs. We can avoid conflicts and also reduce the risks of getting scared, insecure, aggressive and stressed dogs. We also reduce the risk of getting into dangerous situations, being injured and bitten as a result of the dog's self defense.

Story Three - The Hunting Dog

The slim hunting dog stood shivering in the middle of the room–shivering, panting, looking desperate. She was so thin that her ribs stood way out. She was a pitiful sight. Some seconds later the train near the house had passed, and then she started to behave more normally, coming up to greet me, being friendly, as these dogs usually are.

She lived beside the railway, and she was scared to death of the sound of trains when she was inside the house. She had become restless, lost fifteen pounds in a short time, and had developed an abnormal heartbeat.

I was not at all sure what to do. Move to another house? Use drugs? I decided to make a try when the next train came.

I told the owners what to do, and when the faint sound of the train appeared, I sat yawning and stretching "front legs", avoiding eye contact with the dog, but looking out of the corner of my eye to see her reaction. The owners were to look another way, talk normally to each other, drink their coffee. She shivered and panted, but looked at me when I was yawning. She looked at her owners and back again. The panting was not as heavy this time. Could it be possible?

During the next train, everybody sat yawning and did not look at her. There was a positive reaction in the dog.

They got their homework, and I came back one month later. They did not call me during that time, so I know things had not become real bad. I came into the house with the dog greeting me like an old friend. I sat down, and she jumped up in the sofa beside me (allowed!) and curled herself comfortably there, going to sleep. She had clearly put on weight– her ribs were not sticking out anymore. The train was coming, and she looked up at me with one eye, saw that I still was yawning ("that's what I thought") and fell asleep again.

I was speechless and so happy. It was possible to reach through to a scared dog by using her own language, calming her fear. When she had started to become calmer they could also use some fun activities when they knew a train was coming, and that also helped of course.

She was one of my very first clients on whom I used calming signals, so I will never forget her.

I met her years later and she still recognized me. She lived to be an old and healthy dog, hunting rabbits in the forests. And now, I believe, if there are forests in heaven, she is still happily hunting there.

Story Four - Saga

Saga was helping me shovel snow down the farm road, when some people suddenly showed up with two dogs off leash.

The dogs saw Saga and with a roar they both started for her, sounding and looking real fierceful. I started for Saga to get between them, but stopped and let things happen. Saga had already done her job. When they came for her, she turned her back on them and sat down.

It took immediately the energy out of the strange dogs. They slowed down, stopped roaring and started to sniff the ground. They actually never went all the way up to Saga. They stopped at a distance and stood sniffing the ground and being quiet.

Saga did not care for looking at them. Because they were behaving so badly to her, it took any interest for friendship away.

They turned and ran after their owner.

Story Five

The Tibetan Mastiff came with his new owner to me. He asked the dog in a normal voice to sit down, but at the same time bended over him. The dog immediately dropped out, became psychotic, if one can say that, and moved himself from this world to an inner world where no harm could reach him.

These gentle giants with the deep and roaring voices are so misunderstood, and someone had made this dog be afraid of being alive and present.

The dog sat there, completely lost, and the owner tried to pull at him. I asked him to let it be. I went over and sat down beside the dog, looking same way as him, gently stroking his chest with very slow movement, while yawning and breathing deeply.

I sat there for fifteen to twenty minutes, then the dog started to come back to reality, looking bewildered, looking at me, yawning and sitting there still and hardly moving, not a threatening thing in sight. It took him some time to be conscious, but then he licked me, looked at me, apparently feeling safe.

He loved me to pieces after that. I think I could have done anything with him. He had total trust in me and would hardly ever leave when they were here.

It takes so little to be friendly to a dog, and the result can be so overwhelmingly big. You have always a choice of being threatening or calming. To me the choice is easy.

Displacement behavior is to do something else. Is your dog being "stubborn" or "distracted" or just walking away sniffing because you act badly?

Chief Dan George

If you talk to the animals,
   they will talk to you,
   and you will know each other.
If you do not talk to them,
   you will not know them,
And what you do not know,
   you will fear.
What one fears,
   one destroys.

Chapter IV

The Stressed Dog

Stress hormones are necessary for us. We need some quantities of them to be able to work, have energy enough to do things we have to or want to. Sometimes we are in situations that make us scared, upset, very excited or angry. We then get more hormones running around. Then the adrenaline starts pumping.

How it works

You are out driving, and suddenly you have a close accident. You manage, but some minutes later your heartbeat gets faster and you get sweaty palms. You become upset or angry, you feel shaky or thirsty, or you want to go to the toilet. All kinds of reactions will tell you that your adrenaline level is high.

Professor Holger Ursin in Norway has done some stress research (Holger Ursin: *Stress*) that seems to be very valuable to us when thinking of dogs. In his books about stress, you will learn how these things function.

Humans get stressed by accidents, anger, violence, things that excite us–but first and foremost we get stressed in situations where we do not feel we can cope. Something is threatening us, and we are not sure about our ability to manage.

Dogs get stressed for the same reason. They get stressed in situations of threat, of pain or of discomfort. They get stressed when we are angry or punish them. They get stressed by excitement, like male dogs smelling females in season. Lots of full speed action might stress a dog. But first and foremost, a dog gets stressed for the same reason as humans–when they feel unable to cope.

When dogs start to get stressed, they can show it in

many ways. When they are stressed by the environment, you will usually see that they start using calming signals to try to ease the stress. So knowing the calming signals will also help us to see when a dog feels stressed.

Scientific research has given us some more information about stress. In Scandinavia measurements have been done of parachuters, pilots, divers and others who might easily come into situations of danger.

The measuring shows that (1) a situation occurs; (2) five to fifteen minutes later the production of adrenaline is at its peak (that is when we start feeling the heartbeats); (3) parallel to the production of adrenaline two other things start to happen in our bodies: stomach acids get higher and some of the sexual hormones likewise–and these contain defense mechanisms; (4) five to fifteen minutes after the situation that started the adrenaline flow, the stomach acids and the defense mechanisms are at their highest; and (5) then the hormones and acids start going down again. Depending on the environment, the normal level, and other circumstances, the stress level and stomach acids and defense mechanisms take about "several days" to become normal. It is almost impossible to get closer than this.

Pilots with high stress in dangerous situations also had high defense mechanisms–they survived danger. Those with lower degree of stress and defense mechanisms were the ones to die in plane accidents. But the ones with high levels had another problem: they would by time develop ulcers, or other kinds of stomach trouble.

In other words, the stress level together with the activated defense mechanisms are necessary for dogs to survive. They are there to make us react fast enough and be strong enough to survive danger.

It also means something else. A dog with a constantly high stress level will get stomach, allergy and heart trouble. They will be faster and more violent in their defense. They will probably have an activated defense mechanism at a much earlier point than others.

I work a lot with dogs who attack, lunge at people or dogs, and behave aggressively in many situations. Their defense is much earlier activated, they will react faster and more fierceful to things.

It all fits in.

Example One

A dog has a high stress level because of much harsh commanding, high demands from young age, anger and aggressions from the owner's side. The dog is stressed by this every day, and then never gets a chance to calm down.

This dog will also have a very high degree of self defense. He is the one to behave aggressively towards other male dogs, or people.

This dog's aggressive behavior might be learned. It might be slightly inherited. The chance that this is a simple reaction to a life that makes him stressed is very high. His owner's anger and demands make him unable to cope with daily life. He gets stressed. Together with the stress he also gets a much higher self defense, which is the problem the owner in his turn comes to me with.

Very often these dogs die of a heart attack in early age, suffer from serious stomach trouble or so-called allergies.

Example Two

Dogs learn by association. When a dog is being jerked at every time he sees another dog to make him heel or stop barking at the other dog, he will associate other dogs with painful jerks. He will faster and faster be stressed whenever he sees another dog–and faster and faster get his defense mechanisms activated by the heightened stress. This dog will also behave aggressively towards other dogs, often to both males and females.

This leads up to my conclusion: There is no absolutely no reason or excuse to punish, be violent, threatening, forceful or demanding too much towards a dog.

It makes my dog stressed. The stress will by time make him sick. He will easier become aggressive to dogs or people, because he has a higher defense. He might in the end bite someone.

We have always a choice of how to behave. We can understand our dogs calming signals and tell that we understand. Or, we can overlook them and make the dog feel he cannot cope, and thereby make him stressed.

We can behave threatening or in a way that makes the dog become unsure, scared, and in defense.

Some of this defense will be seen as fear. Some dogs have more flight defense, and they will try to escape, look afraid, be nervous or look like it. The fight defense will look like aggression.

When going through some of my enormous material about scared and aggressive dogs, I can clearly see how this fits in.

Aggression, or defense, is a symptom. Very often a high stress level, because of environment, is the cause.

We must try to treat the reasons for the behavior, not only treat the symptom. That will not get us very far.

Look at your dog's stress level. Find the reasons for your dog to be stressed. By looking critically at yourself and your surroundings, you can often find out a lot all by yourself. Sometimes it can be helpful to ask someone to help you see the situation from the outside. We often become blind to what we do.

What makes the dog stressed?

- direct threats (by us or other dogs)
- violence, anger, aggression in his environment
- jerking at the lead, pushing him down, pulling him along
- too high demands in training and daily life
- too much exercise for young dogs
- too little exercise and activity
- hunger, thirst
- not having access to his toilet area when he needs it
- freezing or being too hot
- pain and illness
- too much noise
- being alone
- sudden scary situations
- to much overexcited playing, with balls or other dogs
- never being able to relax, always being disturbed
- sudden changes

Scratching can be a calming signal

25

- not able to calm down, restless
- overreaction to thing happening (for instance the doorbell, a dog coming)
- use of calming signals
- scratching
- biting himself
- biting and chewing furniture and shoes and other things
- barking, howling, whining
- diarrhea
- smells bad, both mouth and also body
- tense muscles–sudden "attack" of dandruff, for instance
- shaking
- change of eye color
- licking himself
- running for his tail
- fur that seems to be hard, breakable, standing on end
- looking unhealthy
- panting
- loosing concentration–can't concentrate for more than a very short time
- shivering
- loosing appetite
- going to the toilet more often than normal
- allergies–many allergies are really stress, scratching
- fixation on certain things–glimpses of light, flies, crackling of firewood
- looking nervous
- behaving aggressively
- using displacement behavior when you ask him to do something

Shaking off can be a calming signal

What can we do about stress in our dogs?

It is not my intention to discuss all the things we can do to release stress in dogs–that would take another book by itself. Here are a few basic ideas:

- maybe change environment and routines

- we can stop using harsh methods, violence and painful things in training and handling, there is no excuse for it, and the dog's reaction to it shows us how valueless it is

- we can teach ourselves to see, identify and use calming signals

- we can avoid putting the dog in a situation of hunger, thirst, heat, extreme cold or keep him from "going" as often as he needs to

- try to find your dog's balance of exercise and activity, too much and too little might be bad

- let the dog be a part of his pack as much as possible, that is be with you or someone in the family, and only gradually teach him to accept some loneliness

- closeness, touching, massage, being tight together without being held by force–lying tight together is stress releasing for puppies, maybe also for your dog

Fear might make the dog more stressed. The stress activates defense, which makes the dog more fearful. Where do we start to break up this bad circle?

> Turid Rugaas: "In many cases dogs become hysterical when I answer them in their own language. It is like someone long lost in the jungle and suddenly at the edge of despair, hears his native tongue being spoken. Maybe that is why rehabilitated dogs remember me years after they have been here."

27

Start by stopping all force, punishment, aggression and anger to the dog. Stop threats and start using calming signals. Your dog will understand and answer you back, and he will feel a lot better by your friendliness. Feeling better is a good start to a new life!

Using a calming signal for your dog

Turid Rugaas: "To be able to communicate, to be actually understood by dogs, that is a wonderful feeling for people and dogs alike. Calming signals are the key and seeing through that opened door has been looking into a childhood dream of talking to the animals."

Chapter V

Your Choice

To you who have been reading this book

It is good enough to read about these things, but most of all I want you to go out there and start watching. The ones who have learned these things from me before, tell me many great stories of how they now understand their dogs better and can help them. They feel they get a better relationship with them, and also they find it exciting and wonderful to observe all the conflict-solving dogs are really doing.

Therefore I hope you will start observing, understand your dog better, and feel closer to the perfect relationship between man and dog.

Until now much of the relationship has been a one-way communication: we demand things from the dog and the dog responds. This is not enough for people who really want to know, who really want to feel relationship with dogs, and being able to understand them. Understanding their language is maybe not enough, but it is a great step in the right direction.

Whenever together with, or meeting a dog, you have the choice: you can be threatening or calming. There is no–absolutely no–excuse for

threatening a dog. It will make the dog defensive, be afraid, not understand you, maybe even in the end do harm to you or others, because his defense is activated.

Dogs are survivors. They defend themselves when they are threatened. Some will fly or try to escape. Others take back. In any case, their relationships with humans are in bad shape.

By telling a dog that you are friendly, you can immediately become his friend, or at least someone he can feel at ease with. It can change your relationship with a dog when you stop threatening and start calming instead.

Dogs are also conflict-solvers, and they try to solve conflicts in their environment all the time. That we continuously start conflicts is really scary to dogs, and it tells them what weak individuals we are.

You always have a choice. It is up to you what king of relationship you want from a dog. He might learn to fear you and live his life being afraid and feeling bad. Or, you can make him feel good, have trust in you, and have nothing to fear, such a dog will hardly ever come in a defensive position and, therefore, is less likely to bite.

In practical handling and training

When you are training down or sit, do not bend over the dog. Bend your knees or keep upright. Maybe side to the dog, if he doesn't like the exercise. Bending over will make the dog move slower, or try not to do it at all.

Do not stoop towards the dog coming to you. In most cases he won't come all the way up to you at all, but will run past you, looking away from you. Stand upright, maybe with your side to the dog, then chances are much higher for him to dare coming to you.

Do not jerk or use a tight leash when commanding your dog to heel. It hurts, it is painful to the neck, and makes the dog try to turn away from you, sniffing the ground or something else. Keep the leash loose–clap your thigh when you want the dog's attention, turn away from him in a right-turn circle, and the dog will follow if he is not dragged along or jerked at. A clap on the thigh, some praise, a turn to the right. That is all it takes, and it is much more pleasant than getting a sore neck.

Do not hold a dog tight. He can learn to accept it, but that has to be done gradually.

The good things are: side to the dog—if you have to get low, don't bend over, but bend your knees instead. Turning away from the dog. Start touching low down, under the dog's chin. Do not hold tight. Never try to hug a dog you do not know very well.

All exercises can be done in many ways. There are always some ways that will be less threatening than others. A dog should not feel threatened while doing things for you. Remember, you always have a choice!

I wish you all a wonderful and exciting time, exploring the language of dogs, and being able to marvel at their ability of conflict-solving and helping each other behave. Dogs are miracles of communication and cooperation–we have a lot to learn from them. My life changed completely from the day I saw how it worked, and even more the day I discovered how I could use their language myself and make them understand me.

Welcome to the world of dogs and to the land of dog language! I do hope you get the same wonderful experiences as I have had. Your dogs deserve it!

"The social dynamics of a wolf pack is often used as a model for dog-dog and dog-human interactions. I have seen dog people (and some wolf people as well) caught up in the idea of always maintaining high rank by aggressive means, believing their only choices are between forcibly dominating the animal or submitting to it. The problem with this approach is two-fold. First, aggression may well escalate, and second, an either-or choice between forcible dominance or submission is not the only choice available to wolves, to dogs or to humans.

With what she calls "calming signals," based on canine expressive behavior, Turid Rugaas introduces dog trainers and owners to another option to try to improve relationships between humans and their dogs and between dogs and other dogs."

Pat Goodmann, Wolf Park

Epilogue

As a five year old I had a great wish for growing up doing "something for dogs."

I did not know what, since I didn't know what there was to do. As years went by the wish only became stronger, and I started on the road that led me up to my own flourishing dog training school and my wish fulfilled.

I feel I reached my goal and even went far beyond it. I hoped for helping dogs in my neighborhood–I have already been to several parts of the world. I train close to 1,000 dogs every year, many of them being helped to a better life. I even got a big money prize for my work with dogs. I believe I must be the only dog trainer that has achieved that.

I also know for certain that the ultimate goal can never be reached. There will always be new dogs needing help, it is a never-ending story. But I know now where my road is winding, and I am more occupied by the road itself than of what is hiding round the next corner.

I feel privileged to be able to do what I have always wanted to do. I will go on doing it until the end of my days, using all my skills, my energy, and knowledge to help as many dogs as I can–doing something for dogs, because they have done so much for me.

Bibliography

Crisler, Lois. *Arctic Wild.* New York: Harper and Brothers, 1957.

Fox, Michael. *Behavior of Wolves, Dogs and Related Canids.* Florida: Krieger, 1987.

Fox, Michael. *The Soul of the Wolf.* Florida: Krieger, 1987.

Hallgren, Anders. *Lexikon i hundsprak.* Koping, Sweden: Jycke-Tryck AB, 1986.

Hallgren, Anders. *Hundens Gyllene Regler.* Vagnharad, Sweden: Jycke-Tryck AB 1989.

Klinghammer, Erich. *Applied Ethology: Some basic principles of ethology and psychology.* Indiana: North American Wildlife Foundation, 1992.

Lorenz, Konrad. *Man Meets Dog.* London: Methuen, 1954.

Lorenz, Konrad. *On Aggression.* New York: Harcourt, Brace and World, 1966.

Mech, L. David. *The Wolf: The Ecology and Behavior of an Endangered Species.* Minnesota: University of Minnesota Press, 1981.

Ursin, Holger. *Stress.* Oslo, Norway: Tanum-Norli, 1992.

The companion video to this book

CALMING SIGNALS
What Does Your Dog Tell You

is available from

Legacy By Mail
PO Box 697
Carlsborg, WA 98324

888-876-9364 (within the USA)
or
360-683-9646